My Holiday

written and illustrated by

Sumiko

Heinemann: London

William Heinemann Ltd
10 Upper Grosvenor Street, London WIX 9PA
LONDON   MELBOURNE
JOHANNESBURG   AUCKLAND

First published 1987
Copyright © Sumiko Davies 1987
434 96541 3
Printed in Hong Kong by Mandarin Offset

It's fun going to bed in the tent.
Mum tucks us in, just like at home.

Next day we go swimming. Dad swings
me around making a big splash. Mum
carries Ned on her back.

I make friends with Michelle. We play
on the beach.

We find a little pool between the rocks.
Ned catches tiny crabs.

We collect some pretty seashells.

Another day we go for a walk in the hills.
Ned can't climb very well.
Dad says I run like a rabbit.

We catch butterflies at the top of
the hill.
But we let them go again.

It's raining. I play in the caravan with my new friends.

One day we go out in a boat. We sail
over to an island.

I play in a rubber boat with Ned. I can
see under the water with a mask.

The water is very warm.

I can see lots of fishes, plants and seashells.

Tonight we have a barbecue.

We cook our sausages and chicken
legs on the fire.

Afterwards Dad helps us light
sparklers. We have to be careful.

How clearly we can see the stars!
Mum tells us stories about the night sky.

Our holiday is over. Goodbye!
It's nice to go back home again.